I can draw!

Princesses, Fairies & Fairy Tales

Walter Foster

Jr.

CALGARY PUBLIC LIBRARY

DEC   2014

D0600532

www.walterfoster.com
3 Wrigley, Suite A
Irvine, CA 92618

Artwork © Fleurus Editions, Paris-2014
Published by Walter Foster Jr.,
an imprint of Quarto Publishing Group USA Inc.
All rights reserved. Walter Foster Jr. is trademarked.
Illustrated by Philippe Legendre
Written by Janessa Osle

Table of Contents

Tools & Materials

Pencil

Eraser

Paper

Sharpener

crayons

colored pencils

Markers

The Color Wheel

The color wheel shows the relationships between colors. It helps us understand how the different colors relate to and react with one another. It's easy to make your own color wheel!

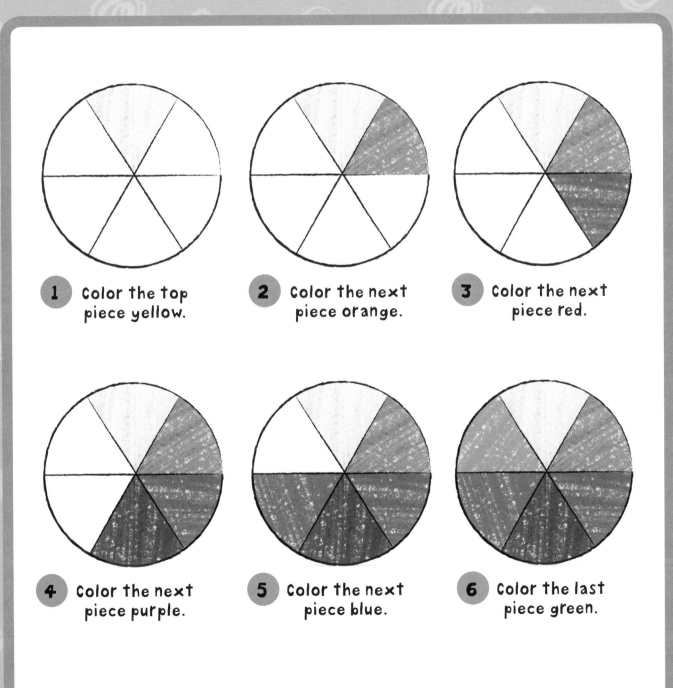

1. Color the top piece yellow.

2. Color the next piece orange.

3. Color the next piece red.

4. Color the next piece purple.

5. Color the next piece blue.

6. Color the last piece green.

Getting Started

Warm up your hand by drawing some squiggles and shapes on a piece of scrap paper.

Draw a square

Draw an oval

Draw a circle

Draw a rectangle

Draw a triangle

If you can draw a few basic shapes, you can draw just about anything!

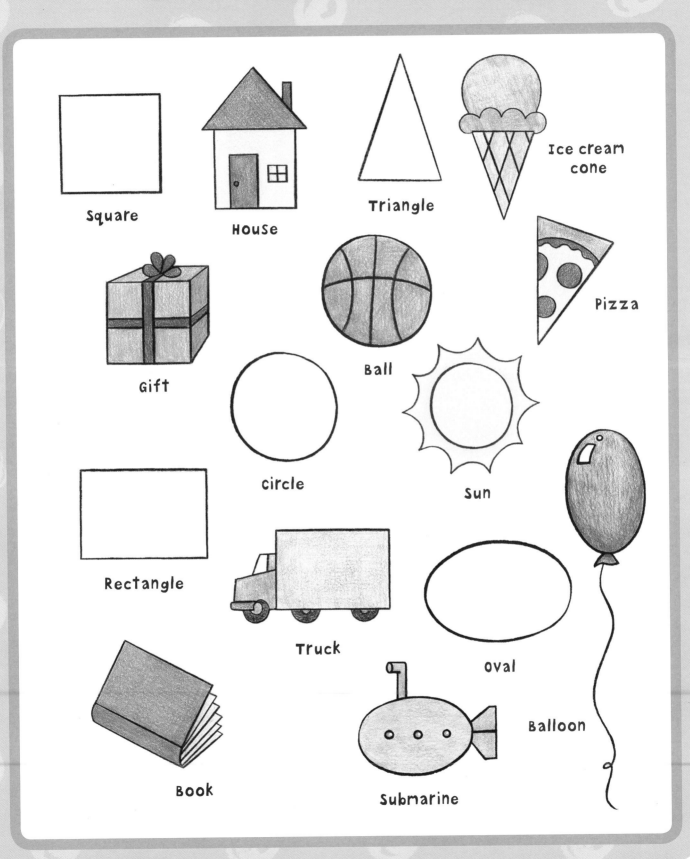

Square

House

Triangle

Ice cream cone

Gift

Ball

Pizza

circle

Sun

Rectangle

Truck

oval

Balloon

Book

Submarine

cinderella

cinderella is saved from a life of servitude by a prince who sees her inner beauty.

Snow White

The fairest in the land, Snow White is watched over by seven dwarfs.

1

2

3

4

Good Fairy

This fairy always uses magic to do good and help others.

Sleeping Beauty

only a handsome prince is able to break the spell that cast this princess into an enchanted sleep.

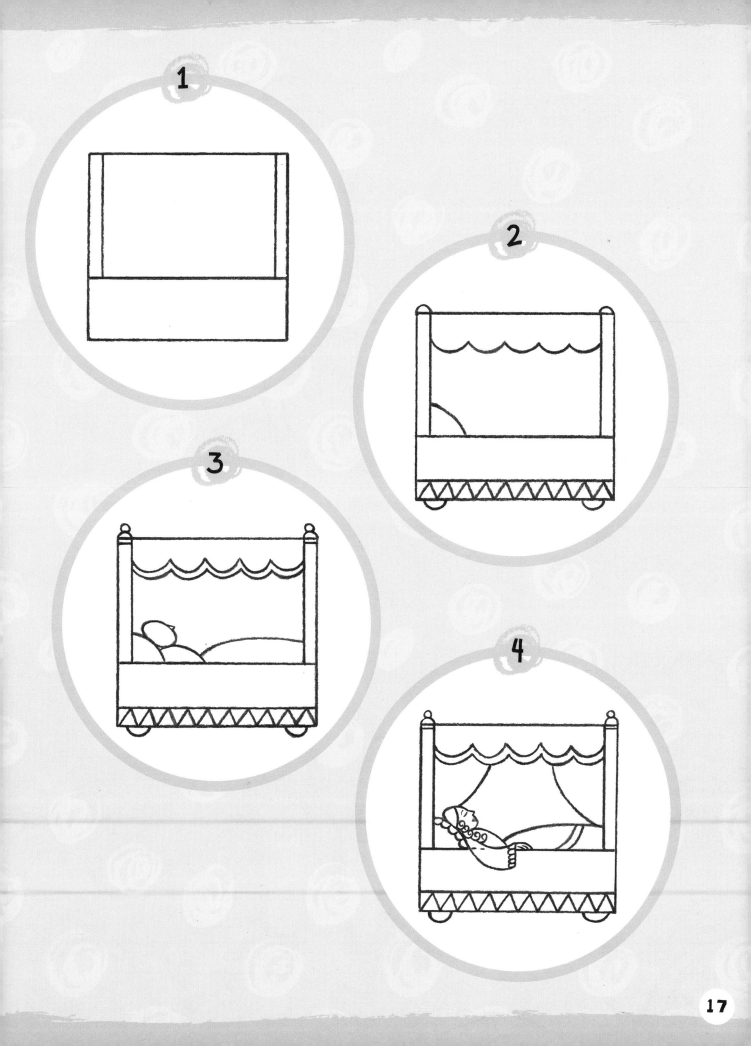

Prince Charming

This prince always comes to the rescue of a damsel in distress!

Dragon

This dragon flies and breathes fire!

King & Queen

This king and queen are good, fair, and just.

Witch

This witch likes to cast spells and fly around on her broom!

Pixie

This little fairy is cheerful and has magical powers!

27

unicorn

This beautiful, magical creature is a symbol of loyalty and grace.

Ogre

This fearsome giant likes to scare people!

Carriage

This horse-drawn carriage is beautiful, elegant, and fit for royalty.

33

Wizard

Wizards are usually wise mentors and practice magic!

Guardian of Treasure

This dragon's job is to protect gold, jewels, and riches from thieves and intruders.

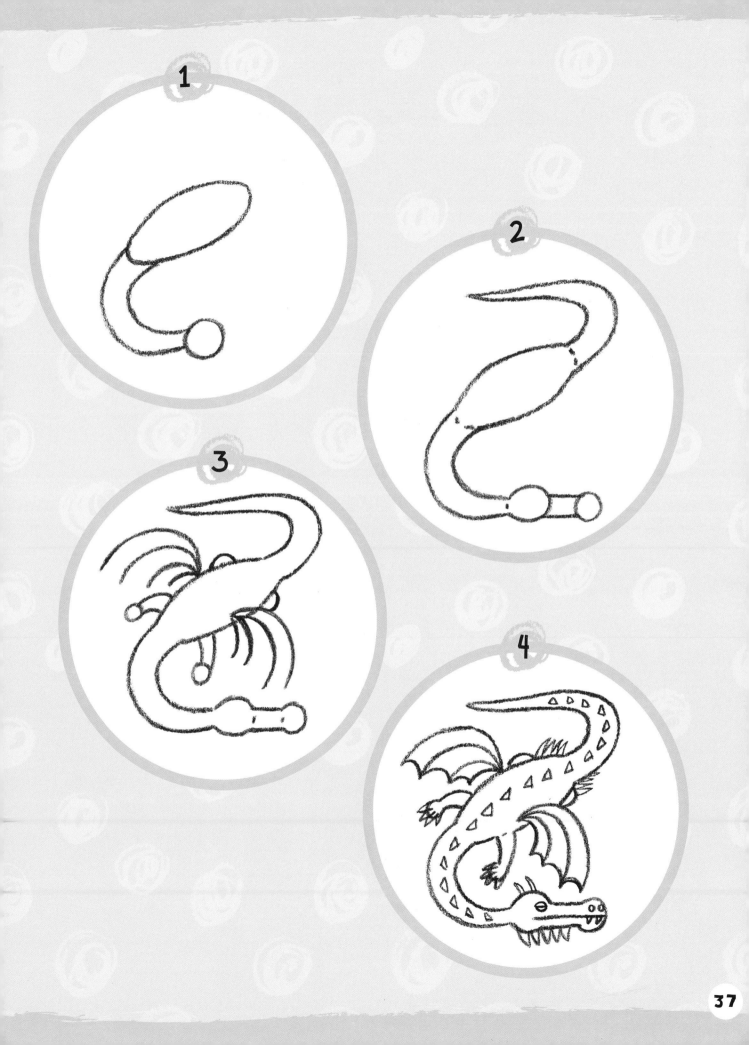

Enchanted Castle

This castle is full of magic, charm, and wonder!

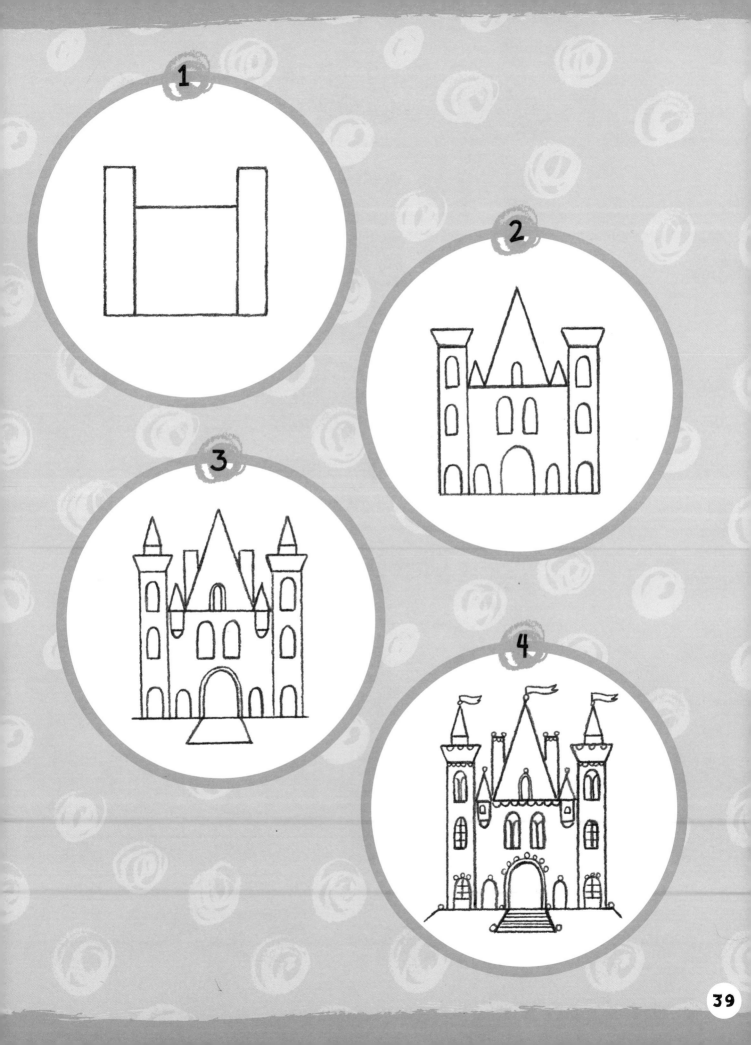

Good Dragon

This dragon uses his magic to do good and help others.

41

Fairy Godmother

This magical fairy acts as a godparent to a prince or princess who needs help.

Elf

Elves are small and have magical powers like fairies!

Mermaid

Mermaids are half-human and half-fish, and they live in the ocean.

The End